The Humanness of You *Volume 1*

Poems & Photographs by Walter Rinder

CELESTIAL ARTS
MILLBRAE, CALIFORNIA 94030

First Printing, September 1973
Second Printing, January 1974
Library of Congress Card No.: 73-86635
ISBN 0-912310-47-2 Paper Edition
Made in the United States of America

Dedication
To my Mom and Dad
Because of you . . .
I feel, I see, I touch, I hear.

INTRODUCTION

I sat on a small fence in a redwood grove
(Richardsons Grove State Park) in Northern California
one early morning in late June. The rays of the sun
were just beginning to penetrate the trees.
The birds had started to talk of the coming
day, and the wind began to stir, swaying
the branches as it moved through the
grove.

This had always been one of my favorite
spots when travelling along the Pacific Coast,
which I did frequently. This time I was alone,
and I wanted to let things happen without
instigating them. I felt at peace with myself,
watching and
listening to life wake up to
the most beautiful of days.

A short time passed, and I heard soft
footsteps on the carpet of pine needles and looked
up to see a young girl walking my way. She said
"good morning" with a warm smile and sat down
beside me. We shared time talking of our lives,
what love meant to us, our dreams, wondering if
we'd have the time or strength to see them through.
She believed we did. That made me feel good. I
watched her get up to go and kissed her on the
cheek. She then took my hand and we embraced
saying in silence what could not be said in words.
In a moment she was lost among the giant trees.

A while later a young boy rode by on a
bicycle, smiling as he waved hello. His face
showed no hate, no fear. His long blond hair
and tanned body looked like he was born of the
sun, a messenger from the universe.

I strolled down to the river helping
two little children catch some baby trout
that were in a small pool. We tried for
some time but they were too fast for us.
Even their parents helped, and we all laughed.
It was fun being together with strangers who
became friends.

The Eel River seemed very warm as my
feet walked over its rocky bottom. I
stopped, looking up at the top of the
redwood trees, and for a few minutes deeply
thought of the perfect harmony of nature and
that I wanted to be a part of that harmony.

A young boy about sixteen years old came up
and asked if I'd like to go swimming with
him. We swam and floated down the river
and dove in a deep pool. We splashed water
at each other and skipped rocks across
the water and then rested upon
the earth. We talked of his friends and their
search for new values, new ways of living, for
their own identity. We both were very open with
each other in our thoughts and feelings. We
related for several hours then he had to go.
The last words he said were, "I wish I had
known you when I was growing up."

The whole day was filled with inter-actions
of people. The inspiration of friendliness
and touching by these human beings filled my
heart with hope, that there is a new beginning.
There was no fear.

Life flowed as it should on this exceptional day.

The two volumes of "The Humanness of You"
represent feelings, human feelings.

Some parts flow, others are scattered, and other poems
follow no particular path of continuity because—

Seeking understanding and ourselves we tread
through a tangled jungle of fulfillments and
joys, conditionings and fears, with little continuity.
This was our heritage, since birth.

We have to clear our own path through this
jungle, thus making this path flow easier for those
who follow . . . our children.

This is what "The Humanness of You" is all about.
Volume II will follow.

Do we give love for giving?
Do we receive love for receiving?
Or are we love
as a flower's fragrance, just is.
Not concerned with a receiver
or a giver.
Just is.

Let us become love.
Let us be love.

HUMILITY OF ABUNDANCE

Let there be those
whose years have honored
their growth,
nurtured by insight,
maturing with wisdom.
Let there be a world
where masters of life share
with youth
the humility of their abundance.
For the apprenticeship of our young
lies with the soul expansion
of their elders.

A person cannot develop
the full extent of his
mind and body unless
his home and surroundings
are in harmony
with his feelings.

Search for this harmony.

FACES OF LIFE

No matter where the highway leads me
no matter where I roam
faces in
a hundred places
drifting in and out of towns, alone

I take the time to share my kisses
to touch a cheek that's tan
their endless dreams
that always seem
to shift through years of changing sand

A face beside a roadside diner
a face beneath a tree
a friendly smile
says stay awhile
is a face that looks intently

A face beside a lighted lamppost
searching for a warm embrace
those lonesome eyes
those desperate cries
is a face without a special place

A face whose beauty swells the senses
churns the feeling of the heart
your soul ignites
emotions flight
is the face the seed of oneness starts

A face held by the morning sunshine
youth's face, tenderly bound
a moment's chance
bares a glance
in shyness, expressing to be found

So faces of my travelled highway
let me love you while I may
I am caring
need your sharing
don't let this precious moment stray.

The world is full of
                    wonders
I know because they
have made themselves
known to me.

CYCLE OF LIFE

Summer's
        almost gone
    the warm days are
    getting fewer

I'm glad summer's
        becoming.

Autumn—for with
   this change my life
   will be different
   with you gone now
   life is bare, as are the
   trees. I am lonely, then.

Winter
          comes
    life rests, getting
    to know itself
    again, as I do, by

SPRING new life finds its place
as will new love, for spring
is a time of sowing
there is much new life as there
is much new love

LIFE WILL UNFOLD TO YOU

Rain clouds teasing the summer's sun
winter playing hide and seek with spring
warm breezes heralding summer's approach
autumn the jester of the seasons

people walking upon the earth's crust
where mountains unknown push above
the ocean's surface
where volcanoes unleash the power
of the earth's core
where lands give birth to new worlds
and love is the air you breathe
life will unfold

BEING TAUGHT

White birch standing in torrents of rain
an old two-story southern house, proud at
watching history unfold
a squirrel scurrying across the house's red tile
roof.
Lightning seen as a memory—thunder heard
clouds, oranged, streaked turning across the
sky like the pages of a great book.
My eyes looking upward, downward, scanning
everywhere as if trying to penetrate the
obvious for a deeper meaning. As I wrote what I
observed and felt, the meaning became simple.
I was being taught.

Love gives flight to all emotions.

"I WANT TO BE HAPPY"

To share life with the meadows,
to smell the tide beneath my feet,
to climb the hills or run upon the valleys floor,
to watch the little creatures make their day,
to see the birth of flowers
and above birds soaring with graceful ease,
to sense the sun upon my body
and feel the rain upon natures brow,
listen to the melody of the stream
and the wind running through the branches,
the lark to wake me from my sleep
and the owl to bid me good night
                    with you beside me.

Nature has given us many gifts
Today I received
a pocket full of diamonds

"DREAMS"

Your thoughts are in the form of dreams!
    a ranch beneath the sky
    your first-born baby's cry
    a girl to build a home
    or a boy's love so together you may roam
    exploring islands upon the sea
    or just lying there, being free.

MESSENGER OF WISDOM

Once appeared a wise man, though a stranger
in my dreams
he came upon a chariot riding down the
sun-lit beams
pulled by celestial horses who grazed
the milky way.
He held the reins of wisdom, in my sight he'll
always stay
his words they echoed loud across the
vastness of the sky
only once, would he share my world,
this his passing by
he took me in his chariot and talked
of many things
showed me worlds beyond my dreams that
would astonish even kings
he said my son these dreams you see are
all within your grasp
if you continue searching and take the
time to ask.

TEACHER OF LIFE

One morning, beneath a spring sun, beside
the gnarled limbs of an old tree, sat an
old man whose white garment flowed as
the wind arose then settled peacefully
upon his body. His eyes wandered slowly
over the countryside, then came to rest
upon the white marble pillars
near the city gates.

The group of young people that surrounded
him were silent, waiting impatiently for
his words. Looking into his eyes they saw
the universe. Each in their own image.
Each felt the space and time
of their dreams.

Presently, the man's attention focused upon
one particular youth and the man began to
speak;

"In all my years I have searched for a man
wiser than myself, yet this man I have not
yet found.

Those that thought themselves wise kindled
their wisdom with false pride and ignorance
                                    I listened

Those that spoke truth within the limits
of their heart did not perceive themselves
to be wise
                                    I respected

Those who made love visible in their toil
thinking not of becoming wise
                                    I followed."

BOOKS AND THOUGHTS

books and thoughts clean the mind
of restrictions built by time
through the pages we discover
all the feelings held from each other
we read the words, think the thoughts
the author expresses to be taught
books to me are like a friend
whose knowledge helps my hurts to mend

darkness is your safety stand
living, haunted, mind of man
your fearful of the light ahead
mind and body stand in dread
from these darken pillars stray
so fulfillment will become your day
learn to live, live to learn
free your soul
       for what it yearns

Feel and see things
                you've never felt before

Ride the seed as it is carried
                by the wind

to unknown places,
                unknown faces

For it will settle somewhere
                upon a spot of earth

And fulfill its purpose.

SCULPTURE YOUR HEART
UPON THE SANDS OF TIME
FOR YOU TRAVEL THIS WAY BUT ONCE

LOVE ME

love me   because I try to touch life
within the framework of uncertainty

love me   in the shadows of my indecisions
as I strive to gain knowledge

love me   in the silence of my hurts
and the noise of my confusions

love me   for the feeling of my heart
not the fears of my mind

love me   in my search for truth
though I may stumble upon fallacy

love me   as I pursue my dreams
sometimes retarded by illusions

love me   as I grow to know myself
even during the times of stagnation

love me   because I seek God's harmony
not man's discord

love me   for my body that I wish to share
with affection, wrapping you in warmth

love me   because we are different
as we are the same

love me   that our time together will be spent
in growing, kindling the world
with understanding

love me   not with expectations
but with hope

I will love you the same.

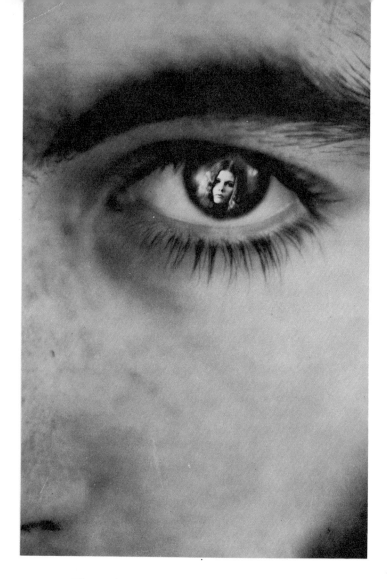

Through your suffering and pain
never lose sight of your concepts and
your seeking of understanding.
Work out your freedom to its
remotest end.
For your life will become
richer when you share each
new found freedom with others.

A SENSITIVE PERSON

Is a human being who is
   not only aware of his own self
   and able to openly express it
   without fear, but is also aware
   of other people's feelings,
   and can relate to that person
   even if the feelings differ
   bringing a more comfortable
   harmony in their relationship.

This is something to strive for
   because sensitive human beings
   project love where we can
   feel and see it.

HUMAN AFFECTION

Sometimes there is no philosophy
    or words to help you
when you're drowning in hurts,
    suffocating in struggle.
So I will jump in and take hold
    of you in silence.
Touch you with my hands.

The most sensitive expression,
    the deepest single communication
of emotion, of feelings, between
    two people is when the mind and
body express as one.
    This we call affection.
It becomes a positive force,
    directed toward the growth
of greater understanding and intimacy.

Affection, expressed openly, is good.
    It eliminates emotional fears,
    frees emotional desires.

TO UNDERSTAND

To be alone, yet not lonely
to be hurt, yet to love
to feel fear, yet not be afraid
to feel change, yet not confusion
is to understand.

AT THIS MOMENT

At this moment he stopped his labor
laying aside his tools
he has in truth
told his friends he wished not their company
has freed himself from the slavery
of commitments and worry
isolated himself from humanity
for in this time of his existence
he has chosen
to spend a portion of time with himself
stopping
just long enough to understand
where he's been
where he is
where he is going

Dear Self:

I've never written you a letter before. Now, at this time of my life, it is important that my mind and body get together in a oneness with all forms of life. So this letter is a reflection of my feelings.

I am aware that my flesh was created through conception of a man and a woman. That my soul was placed into my being upon birth when I became a separate living entity, known as a baby. My mind holds the seeds of thought, my body is the tool where by these seeds manifest themselves into actions and movement, growing in harmony with the universe. All wisdom (the action of knowledge), all forms of love are already within me, only to be opened up or set free by nature's teachings and other human beings who, have themselves, found the truth of their being. Those who live with a loving spirit.

I believe there are universal truths which guide the growth of all living things to their natural fulfillment. Man's truth lies within his soul expressed through his feelings.

Many of man's teachings are in direct conflict to the truths I feel within myself. There is a constant battle between my innerself and the reality of others. When, at times, man's teachings are the same as I feel then the harmony and goodness of my purpose and reason for being a human being are clear. All my struggles and pain and hurts are a learning process which man has inflicted upon me. Fears are like barriers against truth. I cannot run free in life with barriers.

Whenever I can relate to another human being, sharing my body in love and mind in knowledge, I become more fulfilled with myself.

I do not comprehend conscience before birth or after death so my most important concern lies in the realm of human life. As one small particle of the human race, I shall share with all people what my senses encompass, what my learning directs and what my feelings interpret. Life is my teacher, I learn.

Let me feel the humility of wisdom
        and the struggle of ignorance.
Show me the choice of freedom
        and the freedom of choice
the courage of experience
        and the experience of courage
the ability to understand
        and the understanding of ability
the confidence of decision
        and the decision of confidence
the love of man
        and a man of love
I will grow and build my life upon
    those truths my conscience is made aware of,
    for when the love of myself increases,
    (my understanding expands.) My love for others grow.

NEED FOR SOLITUDE

I wanted so much to get away
from my city and its people.
Go out into the countryside
and unwind.
This morning I went skinny-dipping
at Cherry Creek.
The water was so warm
and it was ever so quiet.
Once in a while a child
would laugh out loud
while playing in the water
but other than that I only heard
the sounds of birds and the splashing water
and my own breathing.
The sun wrapped its arms around me
and the wind played with my hair.

We don't need loud music
   or the sound of motors
   or the hum of cities
   or crowds of people
     to feel secure.

POETRY OF LIGHT

I

When you give do not expect
a giving in return
just give because you feel it
then happiness you will earn

II

When I become aware of your needs, trying
to fulfill them, many of my own are at peace.

III

Let your body love
before your intellect controls

IV

To be human
you have to chance
being hurt.

CHILDREN'S VISIONS

Once I could see vast horizons and
    could explore the buffalo plains,
    the deer forests,
    float the length of your rivers,
    ride a horse across your valleys
    and sleep under the stars
        when I was tired

Now your buffalo are gone,
    your rivers are blocked,
    your fences are many and
    your land is no longer free
        to enjoy the night.

I am condensed into your world of
    small designated areas of
    over-crowding and concrete
    as your steam shovel
        eats up the earth.

It's always hungry—as I am, for
    truth and green grass and
    flowered meadows and
    streams I can drink from, and
    earth where I can travel freely
    without another human being telling me
        I don't belong there.

SOUNDS

I'd rather hear the thunderbolts crashing
across the sky
than the ugly sound of diesel trucks as they
come roaring by
I'd rather hear the lapping of a lake
against the shore
than the loud and thunderous buses as they
pass my gallery door
I'd rather hear the morning birds wake me up
from my sleep
than a motorcycle's engine as it yells
and screams and shrieks
I'd rather hear the music as the wind plays
through the trees
or the crashing of the waves as I walk
along the sea.
For I have found a peacefulness in all of
nature's sounds
as man destroys his senses from the noise
that he expounds.

THE NATURAL ORDER

the seasons changing
morning   day   into night
the position of the sun
the fullness of the moon
our feelings toward one another
the growth of love
        all needs—time

EXPERIENCE

Have you felt a grain of sand
         and given it meaning

Have you planted a speck of earth
         and harvested love

Have you taken a blade of grass
         and listened to it grow

Have you travelled with a bee
         sharing its journey

Have you walked the thread
         of a spider's web

Have you watched a blossom
         turn into a cherry

Have you sat upon a mountain top
         seeing the wonderment of earth

If you have, you've begun to see
         the reason for it all

YOU ASK ME

Who I am . . .

    I am a human being. I have seen the vision of wisdom but you have dismissed its meaning as a fallacy.

    I have suffered your reprisals, when my logic and reason directed my actions, imprisoning my time against my will.

    I have felt you pouring me your teachings of love, yet the cup of my soul is always near dry.

    I have desired your knowledge, only to find your concepts and values inadequate and confusing, because I see you destroying human minds and human bodies and living things not of your own kind.

    You ask me who I am
        I don't know
            But I'm going to find out.

This is not the end—but a new beginning.
I am not afraid anymore in the dawn of a new
day for I have felt the humanness of you.

ABOUT THE AUTHOR

Walter Rinder was born in Chicago, spending the greatest part of his youth in Southern California. After two years of college he left home and began to travel in the United States. He now lives in Brightwood, Oregon, under the shadows of Mt. Hood. After traveling extensively in this country he finds this state and its people in harmony to his feelings and growth.

He is Gemini by the stars and greatly holds true to its meaning; a messenger and explorer who collects knowledge and experiences as others collect jewels.

Walter has written four books, this being his fifth, created numerous posters, note cards and parchment writings, recorded his first record album and hopes to extend his talent into film making next year.

His color photography has been exhibited at the San Francisco and Berkeley art festivals, Kaiser Center in Oakland, Elmwood Gallery; Berkeley, and the International Art Gallery in Pittsburgh, Pa. He is very devoted in the art of photography as an expression of his insight in life.

He wishes to touch people with his art, as he touches them with his person. Readers may reach him through This Speck of Earth Gallery, 315 S. W. Morrison Street, Portland, Oregon.